Executive Functioning for Kids 6-12

Simple and Effective Strategies to Help Kids Boost Calmness and Self Control and Get Organized through Executive Functioning Skills

By

IT Publications

Legal Notice

Disclaimer Notice

This book is written and published independently. Please keep in mind that the material in this publication is solely for educational and entertaining purposes. All efforts have provided authentic, up-to-date, trustworthy, and comprehensive information. There are no express or implied assurances. The purpose of this book's material is to assist readers in having a better understanding of the subject matter. The activities, information, and exercises are provided solely for self-help information. This book is not intended to replace expert psychologists, legal, financial, or other guidance. If you require counseling, please get in touch with a qualified professional.

By reading this text, the reader accepts that the author will not be held liable for any damages, indirectly or directly, experienced due to the information included herein, particularly, but not limited to, omissions, errors, or inaccuracies. You are accountable for your decisions, actions, and consequences as a reader.

Table of Contents

Introduction

Our abilities that are responsible for allowing us to make plans, stay attentive, and do multitasking are executive functioning abilities. Executive functioning allows the brain to stay focused and prioritize the tasks to attain objectives. You can understand it by the example of an air traffic controller at a busy airport safely who controls the arrivals and departures of numerous aircraft on various runways.

Ryan is a 4th grade student with executive functioning difficulties. The difficulties do not mean he is not smart, they just indicate the brain's struggles to organize, keeps his emotions in check, and complete tasks.

"Ryan knows he usually forgets something. He forgot his cleats for the game today! Yes! Running back inside to get them, he ultimately forgets his bag there in his hurry to make the bus. He rushes through the school checklist list that his mom had made for him. It is too late, though, as the bus is ready to leave. He will once again miss it.

Ryan's teacher inquires who has the right response to the first question I gave you yesterday on the reading assignment. Ryan tenses, hoping he will not be asked to participate. The questions are not in his planner, and he has no clue how to respond to them.

Ryan loses track of his running direction after he receives the ball in soccer because he is so intent on acquiring it. He moves fast toward the nearest goal and promptly kicks the ball into his own team's goal.

His bedtime has long passed. Ryan is worn out. He tries to sleep, but his brain does not shut off. He continues worrying that his book report will disappoint the instructor and that his friends will make fun of him for kicking the soccer ball into the wrong goal."

That is how Ryan struggles with daily executive function challenges, and your child might be too.

The funny thing is that our brain's frontal lobe controls these mental abilities. Guess what? It does not get fully developed until our mid-20s!

Although no one is born with these abilities, the good news is that our genes do provide a "blueprint" for acquiring executive function. It is essential to establish a responsive relationship with kids through rewarding interactions. It is important to encourage the developing abilities of kids as they mature and provide them chances to apply what they have learned.

According to research, executive function abilities are a better indicator of success in school, the workplace, and later in life than IQ. Also, executive functioning helps kids and teenagers to be excellent students, classroom citizens, and friends. When a person approaches adulthood, these abilities help them balance key responsibilities like family, job, and continued education.

These abilities let us function as effective, conscious, and active human beings. Strong executive functioning enables people to stick to healthy behaviors and minimizes stress.

This book is focused on helping children boost their executive functioning skills with a focus on staying calm and organized. The book is divided into three parts. The first one improves your understanding of the executive function and its benefits, while the rest are for self-regulation, keeping calm, and planning and organizing tasks.

This book will help you to boost your child's executive functioning abilities, a necessary component of content and a productive lifestyle by using simple and tried-and-tested methods.

Let's

get

started!

Chapter 1:
Executive Function: Your Superpower

Executive function problems are common in children who learn and think in unconventional ways.

These types of difficulties are frequently misunderstood. People may believe that children are lazy or incapable of doing more but kids with executive function issues can thrive with the right support.

Let's learn more about the subject.

1.1 Understanding Executive Function

Executive functions are self-control and mental regulation skills that have a neurobiological basis. When developed fully, executive functioning helps adults in achieving their objectives. They can comprehend a problem's nature from various angles, hold several facts in mind at once, plan and rank the steps leading to a solution, concentrate and stay on task, self-regulate and control intense emotions, put up with setbacks, track their progress, and adjust and change directions in order to reach their objectives. The following three main components of executive functioning interact extremely closely.

- *Self-control or Inhibitory Control*
- *Active Memory*
- *Mental or Cognitive Adaptability*

Potential Root Causes of Executive Function Issues

What impairs executive function has been the subject of extensive research. Here are the two main elements.

- *Variations in brain growth: According to various studies kids with executive functioning disabilities have slower development of particular regions of the brain that are responsible for working memory and emotional regulation.*

- *Heredity and genes: Genes play a vital role in developing executive functioning issues.*

Moreover, executive functioning also results in learning difficulties in most cases.

1.2 Myths on Executive Functioning

Myth: Problems with Executive Functioning are Unreal

Fact: It is not surprising that some people might raise an eyebrow at this term. It sounds like an article from a business magazine! But not just CEOs employ executive functioning abilities like planning and time management.

Myth: Problems with Executive Function in Children Resolve on Their Own

Fact: Children do not outgrow brain-based executive function difficulties. Executive abilities can, however, be improved. These abilities continue to increase as children age. Your child's brain can learn how to overcome deficits in planning, organization, and time management by receiving support at school and adopting at-home techniques to build on strengths.

Myth: ADHD and Executive Functioning Difficulties are Interchangeable Terms

Fact: Executive functioning can be difficult for many children. However, not all children with ADHD have executive functioning impairments, and the opposite is also true. While the relationship between the two disorders is still being studied, it is known that children with the inattentive form of ADHD are more likely to have executive functioning issues than children who are hyperactive or impulsive.

Myth: There is Nothing You Can Do About Problems with Executive Function

Fact: There are numerous techniques to assist in enhancing your child›s executive function abilities. To improve your organizational skills, you can experiment at home with various tools, such as visual organizers, checklists, and games. There are things you can do to support your kid›s memory development and flexible thinking. Knowing as much as you can about executive function abilities can help you comprehend your child and determine the most effective ways to support them.

1.3 What's the Catch?

Adults with impaired executive functioning may find it difficult to interact with others, follow instructions, learn new information, concentrate, control their emotions, accomplish goals, and perform well at work.

The underlying components or varieties of executive functions vary. Each performs a significant role, but they also work together on activities with a specific objective. These are:

- **Self-Regulation**

  Self-regulation, also known as inhibitory control, is the capacity to concentrate on a task, control emotional responses, and understand long-term implications.

  For instance, you might experience anxiety when speaking your mind at a lecture or meeting. Self-control enables you to refrain from interjecting.

- **Flexible Thinking**

  Cognitive flexibility sometimes referred to as adaptable thinking, is the capacity to assimilate other points of view and alter thought patterns in response to changing circumstances.

For instance, you might desire to do one assignment but discover that another has a due date that is sooner. You can shift your focus from the first task to the second by using flexible thinking.

- **Working Memory**

   Working memory is the capacity to organize and recall information before being used in another situation or environment. It requires remembering steps in the process and seeing connections between unrelated ideas.

   For instance, when you read a book like a training manual, working memory helps you remember knowledge and provide detailed answers to challenging inquiries regarding the subject.

- **High-Level Executive Functions**

   Higher-level executive functions include reasoning, emotional intelligence, and planning. A person's ability to function successfully in daily tasks, relationships and the workplace depends on their executive functions.

   For instance, they could set poor priorities, overlook resources, or feel frightened by big tasks. Children with ADHD, autism, dementia, or learning challenges like dyslexia frequently experience difficulties with executive function.

- **Focusing on Tasks or Activities**

  A person with low self-control frequently chooses to do nothing or focus on something else instead of the ongoing task. They consequently overlook important information. Due to any attention problem, they might spend more time on one task.

- **Sticking to a Schedule**

  Kids with impaired adaptive thinking needs more time and effort to switch between tasks. They struggle to shift their attention when needed and may develop a fixation on a certain subject or activity.

- **Being Focused**

  People with executive function impairments may experience sleepiness if they must sit still and listen to or read anything that does not interest them. Furthermore, their productivity and problem-solving may be impacted by the speed at which they take in and digest information.

- **Changing up the Routine**

  When an individual struggles with executive function, they prefer sticking with one task to another in a schedule. People regularly experience strong emotions as a result of external cues compelling them to alter their behavior patterns. They might experience sudden, intense emotional overload.

- **Organizing**

   Problems with working memory and self-control may make it difficult for someone to maintain order in their study or employment and establish productive habits. There is also a tendency to lose things. They frequently struggle to distinguish between important and unimportant information.

Let check how executive functioning skills are directly linked to calm behavior.

1.4 Calmness with Executive Function

Interestingly, a growing body of evidence points to executive control impairments in those with high anxiety levels. For instance, several studies have discovered that people with high levels of anxiety, such as those with Generalized Anxiety Disorder (GAD), have a decreased capacity to ignore irrelevant information, particularly when that information is threatening, and have greater difficulty switching attention between tasks. In fact, one of the main signs of GAD is "difficulty in concentrating."

People with high anxiety levels have less psychological room to adapt to new situations since they continuously carry superfluous emotions (their fears). As a result, those who experience high levels of anxiety may be more readily distracted by new information and struggle to transfer their focus between conflicting informational sources (e.g., two different people talking simultaneously).

In terms of working memory, executive functioning permits the mind to concentrate on desirable information while squelching irrelevant or uninteresting information.

That is how executive functioning skills will help your child behave logically and calmly in the face of stress and anxiety.

Chapter 2:
Calm Your Thoughts, Emotions and Behavior – The Angry, Sad and Scared

The emotional reaction to thoughts and actions is a feeling. They serve as markers of how kids relate to a situation. They originate from kids' perspectives and experiences or thoughts.

Kids might behave without thinking while experiencing strong emotions. This can cause them to act in ways they will later regret. For instance, they might scream or curse at someone if they are upset. Alternatively, they can cry or withdraw from people when they are sad.

Let's discuss strategies to regulate kids' thoughts, emotions and behavior.

2.1 Strategies for Self-Regulation

It is tempting to describe difficult behavior as rebellious, attention-seeking, manipulative, and oppositional. However, kids frequently have no control over problematic behavior. When they feel overwhelmed, their emotions take control. They are, therefore, unable to self-regulate.

Self-regulation is the ability to maintain composure, manage intense emotions, adapt, and behave sensibly in various situations. Children who have good self-control perform well at school, with friends, and at home. It makes kids feel good about themselves and what they can handle.

- **Teach About Emotions**

  Start educating kids about emotions so they become aware of the names of things that may initially appear overwhelming. Talking about characters from novels or TV shows can help start conversations about emotions. Ask inquiries like, "How do you think this character feels?" Your child's capacity to categorize their feelings will grow with practice. Even when they are experiencing intense emotions, children with emotional awareness can remain psychologically strong.

- **Set a Good Example**

  Kids learn what they require by observing us. Set a good example by controlling your emotions in front of them and help them become calm and collected.

- **Validate, Validate, Validate**

  Recognize the existing feelings that your child is experiencing. Keep in mind that you are confirming the emotion, not the action. To diffuse the situation, try saying something like,

  "I can understand how angry you are right now," or "A lot of people are terrified and anxious right now — it makes sense that you are feeling that way."

- **Act like a Coach**

  Think of yourself as a basketball coach. You observe one of your players having trouble. The athlete typically makes most of his free throws, but lately, almost none have gone in. You must choose whether to overlook the issue or assist the player in resolving it as a coach. Parents have to make similar decisions. Is it feasible for you to use your kid's difficulties as a chance to teach them and develop a stronger bond with them? Is there a chance to understand and respect their emotions?

- **Study the Five Rs**

There are several methods for promoting and teaching self-regulation. Learn about the "5 R's":

» *Reframe: Encourage the kid to analyze their actions from a variety of perspectives. Kids must recognize their actions and adjust their perspectives accordingly.*

» *Recognize: Know that there are five different types of stress viz, emotional, physical, cognitive (stress from schooling), social (which is frequently exacerbated by social media), and pro-social (the stress people experience when they think about other people's suffering). Kids need to be able to identify these various forms of stress and how each manifests itself.*

» *Reduce: Kids need to develop efficient stress management techniques. They must be able to lower their stress dial.*

» *Reflect: It is important for kids to be aware of and accept their emotions. Many kids cannot describe what it is like to be completely peaceful or identify when they are overly worried.*

» *Respond: Determine whether your kid consistently demonstrates positive self-regulating behavior in your response. If not, look for ways to get them involved in activities that will give them more energy and improve their capacity for stress management.*

- **Build a Coping Kit**

  Your kids might find it useful to gather the materials required to practice the chosen coping mechanisms while you are coming up with a strategy. If they decide to perform a word search puzzle, eat sour candy, and look at photographs of lovely pups, gather those activities and place them in a clear, accessible location that you can guide them to if they are feeling upset.

- **Do not Encourage Outbursts**

  It matters a lot how you react to your child's feelings. Sometimes parents unintentionally support their children's emotional outbursts. It is recommended to stay away from these things if you are trying to teach your kid to control their emotions better.

- **Giving Your Kids Undivided Attention**

  While providing comfort is crucial, be careful not to go overboard. You do not want your kids to learn that acting out in order to obtain your attention is the best course of action. While giving your child comfort might be useful, teaching them the self-calming techniques they will need to manage their emotions without your intervention is crucial.

Let's include some fun activities and worksheets now!

2.2 Activities for Kids to Practice Self-Regulation

In order to ensure that your child can self-regulate when necessary, provide them with meaningful exercises. Here are some games that kids can play to practice self-regulation:

- **Worry Box**

    Pick a box to serve as your worry box. You will store all of your anxieties and anything else that makes you nervous, and it will be locked so that not even the smallest worry may escape.

    Now, pour every bit of stress you are currently experiencing into your Worry Box. Ensure you get everything! Then, firmly lock the lid after carefully closing it. There we go. We no longer have to worry about those concerns because they are now locked up and can no longer trouble us. They are gone! This can be used as an "All Done" box as well. If a child is struggling and continually bringing up a subject, you can place it in the "All Done" box, secure the lid, and let them know it will no longer be discussed.

- **Finger Pulls**

    "Let's attempt to remove the unpleasant sensations from your body. Put all those emotions into your fingertips, and then draw them out of your body as you continue to do so.

> *Place one palm upward and one downward (both facing each other).*

> *Intertwine your fingers, excluding the thumbs. Pull them as far apart as you can.*

> *Hold for long as your body requires (five to ten seconds, at least).*

- **Feel Your Body's Position**

Progressive Muscle Relaxation

When they are anxious, most children stiffen their muscles. Many people even breathe heavily. Kids can learn to use their muscles to reduce the physical stress they feel when frightened by following a straightforward two-step method:

> *Hold a specific muscle group in tension for five seconds, such as the neck and shoulders or the arms and hands.*

> *Feel yourself after releasing the muscles. Work from head to toe to comprehend all the muscles impacted by anxieties.*

- **Taking a Rainbow Breath**

Teaching your kids to "breathe the rainbow," which involves taking slow, deep breaths while picturing their favorite things to go with each color, can help them relax their muscles and lower their pulse rates. To be more effective when feeling worried, practice this technique when kids are calm.

- **My Thoughts do not Control Me**

Fill out this worksheet to develop a positive attitude.

Changing Negative Thoughts

In the red cloud, write some negative thoughts you are having about a situation.

In the green cloud, write some positive thoughts you can have instead.

- **I Understand What I Feel**

This worksheet will help you figure out the reasons you feel certain emotions.

All My Feelings!

Share examples of when you've experienced any these feelings!

A time I felt happy was when _____

_____

A time I felt angry was when _____

_____

A time I felt disappointed was when _____

_____

A time I felt nervous was when _____

_____

A time I felt embarrassed was when _____

_____

A time I felt confused was when _____

_____

A time I felt sad was when _____

_____

- **Move Like an Animal**

  Copy the movement of the animals in a way to understand the feelings of kids at that moment, for example, you can ask the kid to crawl on their stomach like a snake if they are sad and stomp their feet like a grumpy bear when they are angry. kids can also replicate the opposite movement of what they are feeling, for example, moving around the room on tip-toes to replicate the happy feeling. This activity allows kids to understand and change their emotional state and is inspired by somatic therapy.

- **Discuss Scenarios**

  Discuss realistic events that motivate kids to pause and consider how to control their actions. For example, it can be incredibly annoying when someone continually kicks the back of your chair while you are taking an exam. What would you do? You can discuss this question with your kids alone or in a group with their friends.

- **Practice Mantra**

  Consider a recent event that may have left you disappointed, anxious, furious, or terrified. These can be spoken aloud while clapping your hands, while marching to music or while practicing breathing exercises (on exhalation). Here are a few mantras to get you started:

  - » *"I can try another time again!"*
  - » *"I am safe."*
  - » *"No big deal!"*
  - » *"I am awesome no matter what!"*
  - » *"Oh well, maybe next time!"*
  - » *"I am loved!"*

- **The Frozen Dance**

  With a small group of children or family members, have a dance party and instruct everyone to hold still when the music is turned off. The first mover is disqualified from continuing to the next round. The final dancer standing wins.

- **Action and Reaction**

This worksheet will help you avoid negative behavior and think before doing something.

Consequences

Use This Worksheet To Come Up With Agreed Upon Consquences For Behaviors!

- **Sound Safari**

  Ask your child to roam about the home or yard and capture 10 different sounds after demonstrating them how to utilize the phone's digital recorder. Insist that they take their time and attempt to confound you. (An alternative is taking pictures up close with a camera.) Get them back to the couch, which serves as the sound booth, and try to identify the sounds. Pro tip: Discourage "flushing" sounds on your phone to keep it out of the bathroom.

These will help your child regulate their behavior by keeping a cool mind.

Chapter 3:
Know What Needs Your Attention - Work Your Working Memory

Working memory allows us to work with knowledge without any distractions and being sidetracked. Working memory issues can cause the brain to store information in a disorganized way or not even store it for a long time.

Working memory problem is often confused with the attention problem. The brain's storage system never received the information in the first place, i.e., lack of focus. Let's learn about different strategies to boost working memory.

3.1 Strategies for Improving Working Memory in Kids

Does your kid struggle to remember information and forgets about a task while performing another one? Let's learn about some strategies for boosting working memory:

- **Develop Visualizing Abilities**

  Encourage kids to visualize what they just read or heard in their minds. Let's take the scenario where you requested your kid to set the table for five people. Have your kids visualize the table before having them draw it. Kids with the better abilities to envision cannot sketch it but they will describe the image in a better way.

- **Encourage Questions**

  Understanding something is the first step toward being able to remember it. Encouraging your child to ask questions can help ensure that the topic is absorbed on a deeper level. Additionally, it cultivates in kids the capacity for critical thought and problem-solving.

- **Encourage Active Reading**

  There is a good reason why sticky notes and highlighters are so popular: It allows kids to remember the information for a much longer time and enables them to respond to queries in a better way by taking notes and highlighting text. Working memory can also be improved by speaking aloud and posing inquiries regarding the reading content.

- **Give Concise Directions**

  Break down instructions or information that requires more than one step for your child. By doing this, you can ensure that you are not taxing their working memory and that they can take in one idea at a time.

- **Ask Your Kid to Instruct You**

  Organizing information mentally is necessary for performing any particular task. Perhaps the skill your kid is learning is how to dribble a basketball. Ask your kid to teach you how to do this.

- **Allow Your Kid to Come Up with Examples**

  Processing the material is much easier when your kids develop their examples by connecting them to personal experiences. Your kids will retain the information better if you connect the topic in a relevant way.

- **Establish Routines**

  Encouraging healthy activities are one of the best strategies to assist kids in understanding responsibilities. You can establish routine to help your kids in organizing their thoughts.

- **Create Mind Maps**

  Make a mind map of diverse concepts and their connections to one another. Children are more likely to actively engage with the content and gain a deeper knowledge, which is a crucial component of memory when linkages between words and themes are made.

- **Eliminate Distractions**

  Try to reduce distractions, such as noise and sights like TVs and other devices, when your child is attempting to accomplish homework, learn a new skill, or read.

- **Play with Memory**

  To improve recall, use songs, poetry, pictures, and other mnemonic techniques. As soon as they reach home, provide your child with a specific place to keep their keys, bags, sports equipment, and other essentials. Increase motivation to use the system by using a reward chart.

- **Learn Your Child's Limitations**

  The boundaries of their working memory have been reached if you have given your kids what seems like a decent set of instructions, but they keep wandering off course. You can better understand your child's ability to retain information by paying attention to when and how often they start to lose the thread. You can give them useful directions after you are aware of their limitations.

Let's get on with activities for working memory!

3.2 Activities for Kids to Improve their Working Memory

The good news is that various activities can support working memory abilities. Early research was unclear, but a more recent study indicates that working memory may be able to be increased through practice and training.

- **Create a Story**

  Practice making up a short tale with whatever knowledge you need to recall quickly. Use any items or language words to practice this. Let's take the words "bird," "window," "sun," "red," and "smile" as an example.

- **I Went Shopping...**

  The goal of the activity is to recall as many products as you can that you bought at the shops!

  The 1st person to say, "I went shopping to get a ____," names the object they would purchase to begin the activity.

  The 2nd player says, "I went shopping to get a (name of the first player's object) and a ___," and adds a new object.

  As the list continues, players alternately try to recall the products they bought in the correct sequence. The final contestant who correctly names every item in order wins.

By asking players to think of an object that starts with each alphabet letter, you can modify the game for kids who are already familiar with the alphabet. Players 1 through 3 are A, B, and C, respectively.

- **Play Cards**

  Working memory can be enhanced by playing card games like Uno, Crazy Eights, Go Fish, and War. Children must remember the game's rules. They must also keep track of the cards they now hold and those that others have used.

- **Drawing in Air**

  Using your fingertips, create fictional drawings in the air. Since it helps children and teenagers "see" and "feel" what they are doing, this technique can be incredibly helpful for mental math or remembering brief directions.

- **The Letter Game**

  Ask your kid to circle each B on the first day. Start at the top row and work your way down, starting from left to right. Ask your kid to circle all the B's and draw a square around the E's on the second day. You should only provide directions once. Add a new letter and a new direction each day after that.

A B C D E F G H A B

H G F E D C B A G D

E C H D A F B G B E

B D F G A C E H D G

D A H E F B C G G A

G D B A C H E D F B

C H G B E A F G D C

F C A H G D B E B H

- **What is Missing?**

  Put a tray with various household goods on it (the more objects, the more difficult the activity, so for little kids, begin with just 4-5 items and add more with time).

  » *Tell your kids to examine the objects on the dish in detail. Call them all by name.*

  » *Use a cloth to hide the objects. Take one thing out from the tray while asking your kids to close their eyes.*

  » *Allow the kids to open their eyes and take off the tray-cloth to describe the missing item for you.*

  » *Use additional items and give older kids a minute to examine each one. Then, hide them and instruct them to draw or write about the object they just saw.*

- **Sequences of Numbers and Letters**

  You might want to try starting with a small number sequence and building it up digit by digit. Give kids a minute to go over it before taking it away completely. Before the process is repeated with letters, the kids might try to retain as much of the order as they can.

- **When was the Last Time?**

  Give kids recall-based questions to answer. For example, when was the last time you drank lemonade, tied your shoe, made a paper airplane, or changed the volume on something? Kids can record their responses in journals or discuss them with other kids.

- **Repetition and Repetition**

  Children should be encouraged to memorize data in their long-term and short-term memories by repeating exam questions, learning times tables, and reviewing vocabulary cards.

- **Remember and Draw**

  Allow your kid to look at the following drawings for a few moments, and then ask them to draw the missing parts of the items at the end of this chapter. You can increase or decrease the items to make this game easier or harder.

- **I Took a Trip to the Moon and…**

  Kids can play this game at home, but it is always better to play this game in a group to make it more interesting by adding different personalities to the group. The first participant begins the game by saying, "I went to the moon, and I took a…" and then chooses an item to bring with them, like a "pencil."

  The next person will follow the first statement and will include another item, for example, "I traveled to the moon, and I brought a pencil and a cup." Each player keeps adding more items and kids should recount the items before taking a turn. Choose a starting sentence that will appeal to your kids from options like "I went to the museum and I…" or "I went to the market and I…" to play this game. As kids recollect the lists, the game's repetition helps develop their memories.

- **Drumbeat**

  To play drumbeats, use pots and pans that have been turned over or drums. The first player gives the beat by beating their drum and the second player has to replicate it on theirs. Kids can create the rhythm by taking turns. This game helps kids develop their listening abilities, which are crucial for learning to read and write because they exercise the auditory processing system and create the groundwork for understanding diverse speech sounds.

- **Do you Remember Me?**

Complete this activity by writing a favorite memory of each loved one.

Favorite Memories

Write down your favorite memories of your loved one. Why is each memory special to you?

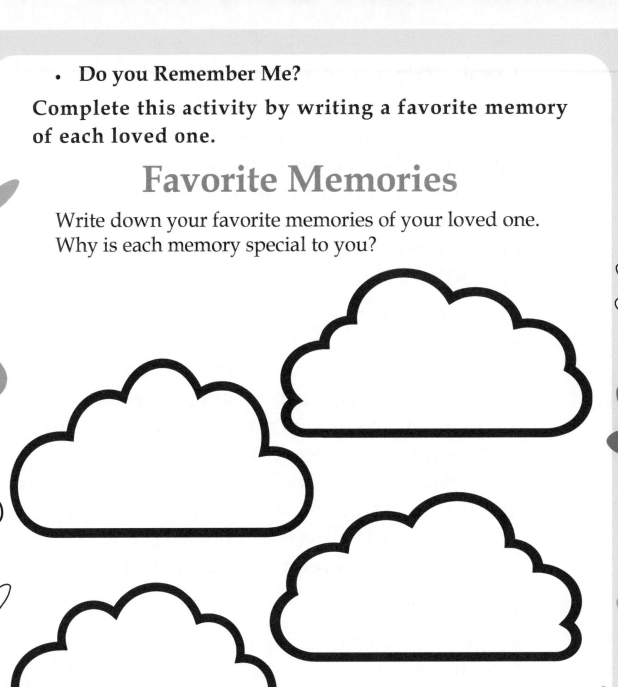

- **Remember and Draw**

  Here is the practice sheet for the "Remember and Draw" game.

I hope you enjoyed these activities!

Chapter 4:
Design Your Happy Days – Plan and Concentrate

There are so many things to keep in mind, balance, and keep track of in this modern hectic world. Even young kids have a lot of information to manage, especially since their attention spans constantly change as they go through their early developmental stages. This is particularly challenging for young kids who are still learning the skills necessary to recall and manage everything on life's ever-expanding to-do list. That is why they need focusing and planning skills.

Focus and self-control require the growth of executive functioning abilities, such as paying attention, learning and remembering rules, and resisting acting on the first impulse.

When a kid learns to plan, this skill will help him/ her to achieve the goals more effectively. It is always beneficial for kids to plan a task before starting.

Let's include some strategies for both subjects.

4.1 Strategies Toolkit for Planning and Concentration

Similar to muscle, concentration needs to be exercised regularly to grow stronger. While some children are "stronger" in this area from birth than others, all children can acquire techniques and partake in activities that will enhance their capacity for sustained attention and focus. Most kids can focus on entertaining things that they will ultimately appreciate. The tasks that are more tedious, challenging, or simply less appealing really test their ability to concentrate.

- **Take One Thing at a Time**

  Multitasking impairs the focus, that is why ask kids to do one thing at a time. You might simply sing the alphabet aloud to very young toddlers while pointing out the letters. You can work on one long-division issue at a time with kids who are a little older, like 4th graders.

- **Just Give One or Two Instructions at a Time**

  Children with trouble focusing may find it challenging to listen to, remember, and carry out instructions. Therefore, try to avoid giving your kids too many instructions at once.

- **Establish a Goals List**

  Kids occasionally struggle to focus, but sometimes it is because they are unsure of what to focus on. Make a list of objectives before your child begins any homework or a study session to offer them direction. For instance, if your child is starting a study session, one of his or her objectives would be to go over and make study notes for a single chapter or topic. Once your child has accomplished these objectives, give him or her a break so that they can rest their mind before beginning a new work.

- **Fix a Due Date**

  If your child is not given a deadline for their homework or does not create one themselves, it might not get done. Your children will benefit more from the idea of setting deadlines for themselves than from having deadlines imposed on them by others.

- **Learn to Observe Things as They are Happening**

  Although a child's creativity is a good thing, they should be able to concentrate and block out distractions. You can play the game "I spy with my little eye" and take turns observing various items in the room, pay special attention to a song's lyrics as a group, or perform some yoga positions.

- **Be Open to What Works**

  To concentrate, some people require complete silence. Others benefit more from loudness. Asking kids what works best for them is crucial because of this. Perhaps your kid wants to play music while doing their homework. Try it out and see how it turns out.

- **Get a Calendar**

  Start by giving your kids a place to record their intentions in writing. It can be done with a planner, calendar, or notebook. Simply provide your kids a spot to schedule their days, weeks, and months.

- **List Everything**

  Make a list with your kids for the upcoming week. Include work from school and house chores. Try to avoid the impulse to do it yourself as you guide your child through this. The only way to reinforce the skill is to let your kids perform it.

- **Talk About It**

  Tell your kids how doing this will benefit them. Inquire about their feelings. Do they require assistance with anything in particular? Discuss their fears and stressors for making a plan to deal with them together.

- **Set Schedules and Priorities**

  With the list in hand, assist your kids in prioritizing and scheduling the most crucial tasks. Do not forget to include entertaining items that cheer up your child. Enjoy doing this. Allow your child to decorate their planners with stickers and uplifting words. They will feel less anxious and happier while doing this.

These strategies will help your child plan well and focus on their tasks efficiently.

4.2 Activities Toolkit for Planning and Concentration

You may be underestimating how capable your young child is. Empower your child with important planning skills and focus on their tasks so they can be more independent.

- **A Day Out**

  Have your child organize a day trip or other outing, and help them decide what will be required. For instance, if your child wants to visit the zoo, you might suggest that they print a zoo map from the computer and rank the exhibits they want to see when they arrive.

- **Mazes**

  You can find mazes that are suitable for your child's age. Start with the simple ones and work your way up. Observe their pace and mistakes. Of course, remember to acknowledge rising marks. Mazes are excellent for increasing processing speed, planning, focus, and visual-motor integration.

- **Make Homework Easy**

  Create a consistent plan for your family and incorporate homework into it. If necessary, split the homework period into two blocks (after school and after dinner) and get your child to plan what they want to do in each block.

- **Make a Basic Meal**

  Invite your kids to assist in meal preparation, and try your best to maintain composure as flour spills and eggshells fly. Here are some suggestions for introducing young kids to cooking:

  » *Teach children how to make smoothies and sandwiches.*

  » *Let them try the toaster oven.*

  Your kids should be able to use the stovetop under supervision by age 10 if you steadily build upon their developing culinary skills.

- **Chess**

  One of the most well-known games in the world is chess and for a good reason. This game is the ideal afternoon diversion to promote strategic play and increase one's attention span.

  Even after only six months of experience, evidence indicates that playing chess helps to improve focus and attention.

- **Head-Toes-Knees-Shoulders**

  You will be familiar with the song Head, Shoulders, Knees, and Toes. It is a fantastic tool for instructing children in focus and concentration.

  Touching the body part listed in the song is a natural reaction. However, studies have shown that instructing kids to do the opposite of what they are taught—for instance, touching their toes when advised to touch their head—helps them learn to focus.

- **Day and Night**

  Kids are instructed to say the opposite of what is written on a card (or picture) in the day-night task. For instance, kids are expected to respond "day" when shown a dark card with stars. Researchers have been using this technology for years to help kids focus better.

- **Plan it Out**

  Help your child make schedules and to-do lists using this planner below!

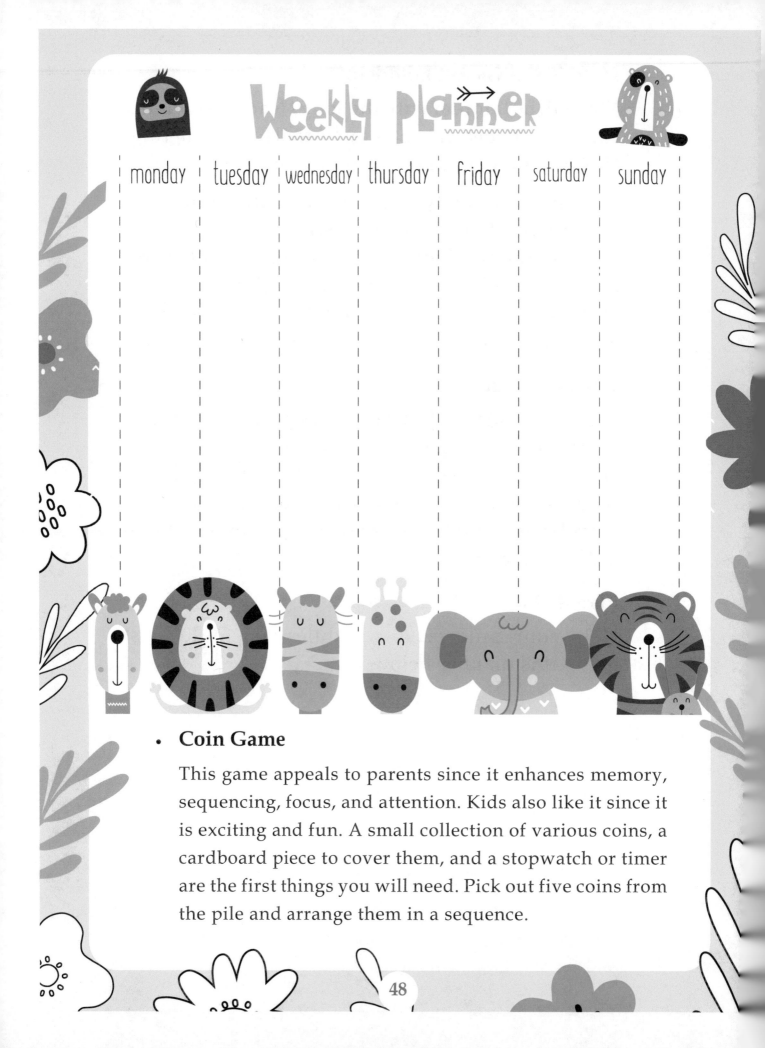

Weekly Planner

monday	tuesday	wednesday	thursday	friday	saturday	sunday

- **Coin Game**

This game appeals to parents since it enhances memory, sequencing, focus, and attention. Kids also like it since it is exciting and fun. A small collection of various coins, a cardboard piece to cover them, and a stopwatch or timer are the first things you will need. Pick out five coins from the pile and arrange them in a sequence.

Instruct your child to look closely at the coins piled on the table. After that, put the cardboard over the coins. Set the timer, then instruct them to use the coins in a pile to create the same pattern. Mark the time with the timer when they are finished, then take off the cardboard cover.

Note how long it takes them to finish the design and whether they are accurate. If your kids do not finish it properly, encourage them to try again until they can. You can make the patterns more challenging as you proceed by adding nickels, pennies, quarters, dimes, and half dollars. As they play more, you will see your child's focus and sequencing skills advance, which is a wonderful reward for you.

- **Draw a Mandala**

  A mandala is a circular abstract pattern with equally spaced patterns that evokes a sense of harmony and balance. Mandalas are a fantastic art therapy tool for relieving stress in children and improving focus.

- **Body-Mind Integration**

  Have your kids try to sit on a chair without moving as an illustration of this method. The parent calculates the child's maximum endurance time. Improvement can be shown after several weeks of practice. This activity strengthens the neuronal connections between the brain and body and helps in enhancing self-control.

insects I SPY

- **Play with Stories**

  You only need a decent narrative book and a creative mind to play these activities. You can just read the kids a brief story and then quiz them on it. Alternatively, you may give your child a paragraph or two from a story and then ask them to predict what might happen next.

  Give instructions on how to maintain the content's connection to the original story. After your child has described what he believes will occur next, you may then give your perspective. Continue bartering back and forth as much as you can to see what they can come up with.

  These games improve concentration and working memory. Additionally, they can aid in the growth of reason and comedy.

- **Ball Paddle**

  Did you ever use one of these to play with? Its simplest form consists of a wooden paddle with a rubber ball fastened to it by a rubber band. The equipment is simple to locate at a toy or drug store.

  It is best to begin with bouncing the ball downward and, once you have mastered that, move on to bouncing it upward. Record how long your kid can continue to make the ball bounce. Encourage extended duration. To motivate children, you might wish to discuss what it would take to break a record.

- **Regular Workout**

  Exercise has been shown to improve a child's ability to focus. It boosts a child's energy and aids in memory, attention, mental clarity, and mental sharpness. It also helps to reduce anxiety.

  Make sure your kids are moving about. The easiest approach to accomplish this is to promote frequent unstructured play, particularly outside.

- **Puzzles**

  All ages can benefit from puzzles as excellent concentration drills for kids. Kids' focus and concentration skills significantly improve due to their commitment for the task.

- **Relaxation and Optimistic Thinking**

  The brain can develop new skills when simple relaxation techniques, such as deep breathing, are combined with helpful mental imagery. For instance, studies have shown that when someone trains their golf swing mentally, their brain records the fictitious trials just like the real ones, which helps them get better on the course.

Work together with your child to complete these mental activities while acting as their coach. Encourage them, and as they advance, monitor their development. Working together is the best action because it improves your relationship with your child.

Go ahead and enjoy yourself with your kids while doing the activities. Who knows, you might even discover that your kids' brains are a little sharper and faster than yours!

Chapter 5:
You are a "Goal" Keeper – Be Organized and Time-Efficient

Organization is the skill that enables a child to tackle problems in a systematic way. Being organized means being able to gather all the provisions needed to do a task and taking a step back to analyze a complicated situation. When a child takes the time to gather all of their notes before beginning to prepare for a test it demonstrates his or her organizational abilities.

Time efficiency plays a significant role in having an organized lifestyle. Children can be prepared for success by learning time management as a life skill. For children to succeed in their education and other aspects of life, they must learn at a young age. Managing one's time effectively might help one to focus on their objectives and complete work without feeling overburdened. Kids with the ability to manage time properly can increase their self-assurance, organization, and learning capacity. Let's head onto the strategies for learning these crucial skills.

5.1 Strategies Toolkit for Developing Organization and Time Efficiency

Developing organization and time efficiency can need some work at first, but it will pay off in the end. Here are some suggestions to help kids become more organized at home and school.

- **Give Them Tasks that Need Categorization or Sorting**

  Cleaning out a closet, organizing your socks and shoes, emptying the dishwasher, and other tasks that require planning, writing lists, or arranging things are all excellent activities.

- **Teach Them How to Make the Most of Their "Free Time"**

  Children occasionally have a lot of free time, such as when they are on vacation. Learning efficient time management skills will be essential for them later in life, especially in college when attendance requirements are only 10 to 15 hours a week. Three actions make up time management: planning, prioritizing and estimating the amount of time needed.

- **Make a Timetable**

  Assist your child in developing and adhering to a timetable for homework, playtime, housework, extracurricular activities, and learning new things. Review the outcomes after a week. Your kids will better understand time management after a few modifications and an ideal schedule for managing their leisure time.

- **Maintain Organized Notebooks**

  Put all the papers your child needs to keep track of in a binder or notebook. They can review the information for each class day using this and organize the material later to prepare for exams and quizzes. To categorize class notes, use dividers or color-code your notebooks. Worksheets, notices, and items for parental signature can be arranged in separate "to do" and "done" folders, which can serve as a central location to keep completed assignments.

- **Make Managing Time Enjoyable**

  Adults frequently connect time management with PTA (Parent-Teacher Association) meetings, countless appointments, bedtimes, and carpools. You might want to hurl the clock out the window due to the tension.

  Kids should enjoy learning time management. The best way to let kids enjoy learn time management is to encourage them to make their own calendars by putting stickers and marking key days with colors and crayons. Kids can also make daily routine duty charts to compete with each other to see who can finish tooth brushing or preparing backpacks the fastest. Kids will learn time management more efficiently if you can make it more enjoyable for them. If they enjoy managing their time it will be simpler to teach them the value of time.

- **Establish Routines for Your Home**

  Setting up regular schedules for meals, bedtime, playtime, TV time, and other activities will help your child develop a stable routine and feel rested each day. They can also learn what to expect when particular tasks are scheduled for specific days.

- **Praise Effort**

  When your kids demonstrate strong organizing abilities, compliment them. Praise is a good technique to support your child's efforts to establish a pattern for the organization because kids respond well to it. Additionally, some kids will have difficulty mastering organized skills and need encouragement to stay motivated.

- **Use Alarm Clocks**

  Avoid waking them up for school, calling them late, or picking them up from home if they miss the bus. Interesting alarm clocks that can roam around the room and out of reach of the snooze button are available in the market.

- **Color-Code**

  Give color to each academic subject. For arithmetic, use blue notebooks and folders, and green for English. Use colorful pocket folders to organize documents that need to be signed and returned. To assist children in transitioning from the position of the writer to the role of self-checker and editor, suggest using pens of various colors.

- **Maintain Weekly Cleaning**

  Every week, let kids go through their book bags and notes. Old exams and papers must be categorized and saved in a different file at home. Papers, packaging, and other waste should be disposed of. Student's school supplies should either be in a designated pocket or back in their home study area.

- **Use Storage Bins and Shelving**

  To keep goods of a similar nature together, use organizers and containers. By doing so, the kids learn where to look for things and how to put them back at their proper places to prevent losing them.

- **Instruct Them on Time Estimation**

  Making a schedule is one of the simplest ways to perform action analysis, a requirement for scheduling. Give your child a day to practice following their schedule. Spend 15 minutes every day at the end of the day reviewing what you did. You can evaluate time, work-related progress, and output. Any alterations should be reflected in the timetable for the following day. This will help your child's estimate skills.

- **Set Priorities**

  Knowing what needs to be done or should be done is helpful. For instance, if your child attends a remote school, be sure to talk with the teachers to determine the key areas that require attention.

Develop a routine that will make sure enough time is put aside after talking with your child to assist them in understanding the significance of each chore. Discuss these goals with them and let them know that you can adjust your schedule so they have enough time to concentrate.

- **Make Sure They Understand the Consequences**

Being accountable for your actions is a crucial aspect of time management. Otherwise, it can cause tasks to be delayed or fail, which might affect other activities. By giving them a task, you may ask them to be responsible. Then, you can explain what would happen if they didn't do it right. Additionally, assist them in understanding how to enhance their abilities.

- **Recognize their Anxiety**

Tell them you are there to assist them at any moment if they have a problem with the plans. Consider their issues and come up with solutions. To prevent stress in your children, do not press them to complete any tasks and refrain from being overly stern.

- **Do not Over-Schedule**

One of the parents' biggest mistakes is getting their children involved in every activity after school.

Nowadays, all kids experience is a never-ending state of go, go, go, which makes them want a few moments of downtime rather than learning how to manage their time effectively. Their clock and yours are both thrown off by overscheduling. Try to avoid it so that everyone can improve their time management skills.

- **Employ Kid-Friendly Time Management Applications**

Tools that are simple to understand may be needed for children. They find visuals to be considerably more enticing. Sit down with your kids and make one on your own if you cannot find any outside. Examine their calendar and devise inventive but visible ways to help them learn and manage their time.

These strategies will help your child to be organized and time efficient!

5.2 Activities Toolkit for Developing Organization and Time Efficiency

Children who are well-organized perform better academically. They stay on top of deadlines and class schedules, manage assignments, take good notes, and maintain orderly bags. Chronically dirty rooms, a propensity to misplace schoolwork, overlook assignments, and begin projects without the necessary materials all indicate poor organizational abilities in kids.

Fortunately, there are lots of enjoyable things that you can do at home to help your kids become more organized.

- **Plan an Event**

  Give your kids the responsibility of planning a family movie night, weekend event, or informal gathering. As you go over the specifics with your child, let them take the lead in selecting the attendees, snacks, food, and the time and date. Describe how planning things before time results in a better experience overall.

- **Clean Your Room**

  Kids can plan to focus on cleaning and de-cluttering their room using the following worksheet.

Clean Room Check List

GET READY....

Get a trash bag, kid-safe cleaning spray, microfiber or paper towels, and vacuum cleaner

GET SET....

Put on some tunes or podcast to keep You motivated

GO....

Check off each task and soon you will have a clean room!

STEP 1

- [ ] Put dirty clothes and towels in hamper
- [ ] Bring empty cups and dishes to kitchen
- [ ] Throw away trash

STEP 2

- [ ] Put dirty clothes and towels in hamper

STEP 3

As you clean up, put everything back in its 'home' and make a pile of items to go into other rooms.

- [ ] Clear your floor
- [ ] Clear your desk
- [ ] Clear your nightstand
- [ ] Clear your dresser

STEP 4

- [ ] Dust and wipe down flat surfaces
- [ ] Vacuum or sweep your floor

STEP 5

- [ ] Put items away that go in other rooms
- [ ] Throw away trash bag
- [ ] Enjoy your clean room!

- **Scavenger Hunt**

Keeping track of your possessions is crucial when organizing. You will be able to visually see what you should keep and what you should think about getting rid of. There are many choices to be taken about an outdated swing set and the rusty tools you used to construct it. Scavenger hunts for decluttering may seem unusual, but they could be one of the most effective methods for including everyone.

At any age, scavenger hunts are a blast. Indeed, even for grownups! An inventive tactic is to conduct a scavenger hunt throughout your home using the items you are trying to organize. Who would not appreciate organizing and bonding all in one exciting detective game?

> » *Start by deciding which areas of your house you wish to organize or clear.*
>
> » *For instance, you might decide to clean your child's closet of out-of-season clothing or reorganize their stuffed animals.*
>
> » *Come up with puzzles that give the impression that the participants are detectives looking for the next component of the puzzle.*
>
> » *They will follow your hints to the locations you want them to get in shape.*
>
> » *Together, we must organize and simplify in order to discover the next clue.*

Everything will be in its rightful position once all the hints are discovered! Make sure a reward waits for them after their work since they solved the case.

- **Flip Your Home Upside Down**

  Room reorganization and garage or basement cleaning are two organizational tasks you might choose to complete with your kids. Ask your kid for his or her suggestions on how to arrange these spaces best. Think of items like shelves, baskets, hooks, or other equipment that will be useful for arranging the stuff while you brainstorm with them. Additionally, encourage them to consider how various elements might work together. For instance, if you are cleaning the garage, it can be helpful to designate one area for water activities, another for gardening tools, another for sports equipment, and so on.

- **Prioritize with Me!**

Urgent, Important....It Can Wait!

What are some things you need to get done?
What is urgent, what is important and what can wait?

Use this worksheet to help you prioritize what you need to do

What are some things that need to get done as soon as possible?

URGENT!

What are some important things that need to get done, but not right away?

IMPORTANT!

What are some important things that need to get done, but not right away?

IT CAN WAIT!

- **Start a DIY Project**

  Another suggestion is to set up a "Do It Yourself" children's corner or Home Depot. Your kids naturally learn how to finish a particular project in these spaces. They will better understand the organizational elements required to complete these constructive projects by discussing their experiences afterward.

- **Plan a Charity Event**

  Help your kids sift through old toys and decide which ones they want to keep and donate. Encourage them to consider how having all of a toy's parts and even grouping toys are enjoyable to play with. Even better, your kids might opt to set aside a spot in your home for storing outdated toys that will eventually be donated.

- **What is a Minute's Length?**

  » *Bring the child(ren) to a space without clocks (or where all the clocks are covered).*

  » *Remove their watches and phones.*

  » *Tell them to sit up and close their eyes. Then instruct them to open their eyes once they think 60 seconds have passed.*

Some children will open their eyes before the allotted 60 seconds, and others will do so later. By learning how effectively they perceive time in general, this game will help kids to more accurately estimate the time to complete activities and projects.

- **The Jigsaw Puzzle**

    One of the exercises used in time management classes that teach participants the value of knowing what they want before deciding how to spend their time is the jigsaw puzzle.

    » *Divide kids into groups of three to five in each. Give each group a puzzle but DO NOT include the large picture image so that they cannot see the final result of the puzzle.*

    » *Stop the process after three minutes and inquire about what is lacking. What makes solving the puzzle challenge? They will probably claim that it is because they are unable to perceive the overall picture they are aiming for.*

    » *Give them the big picture now, and they ought to finish the puzzles much more quickly. The lesson of this time management training game is that it is very difficult to perform effectively and promptly without knowing our ultimate objective.*

- **Dirty Desk**

Keeping your desk tidy is a very important job!
Sam has a very dirty desk!

Inside his desk he found these things:

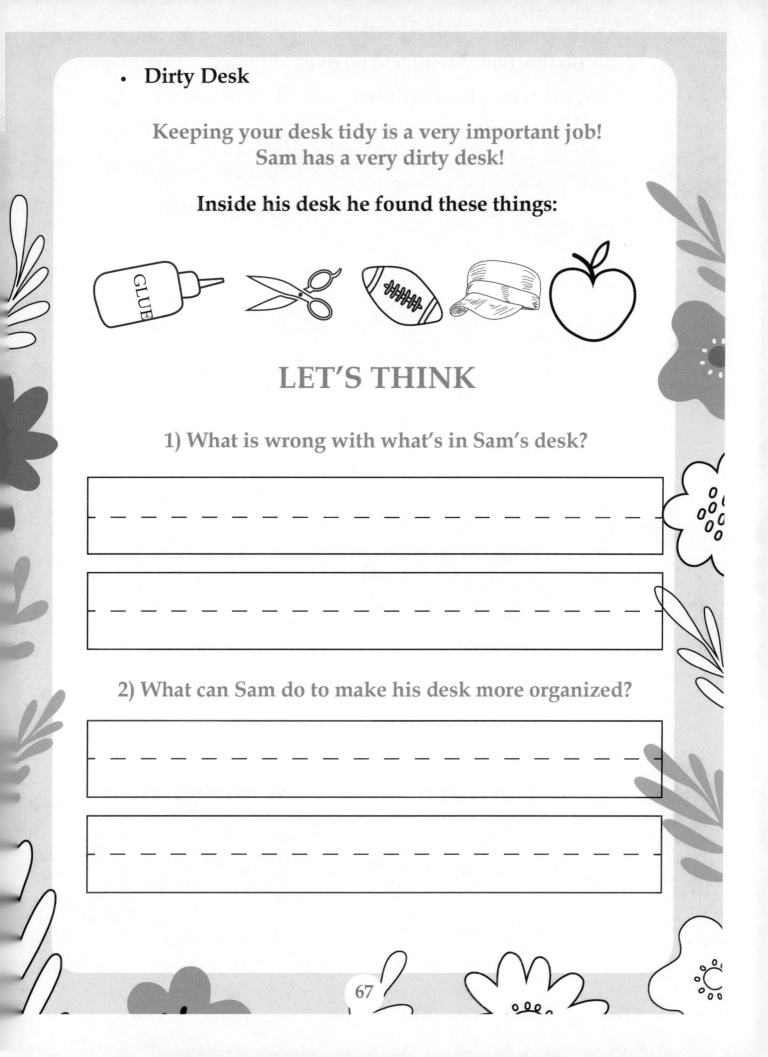

LET'S THINK

1) What is wrong with what's in Sam's desk?

_____

_____

2) What can Sam do to make his desk more organized?

_____

_____

- **Be Precious About Your Time**

This worksheet will help you divide tasks for the day and so much more!

DAILY PLANNER

DATE

SCHEDULE

PLAN FOR TODAY

NUTRITION

NOTES

IDEAS AND THOUGHTS

DAILY HABITS AND GOALS

- **Bright Crayons**
  - » *Purchase a set or two of colorful crayons.*
  - » *Each color should be given points.*
  - » *Ask the kids to collect the crayons at the beginning of the one-minute time limit to get the most points.*
  - » *According to the guideline, they are only permitted to use their dominant hand and one crayon at a time.*
  - » *This game trains kids to concentrate on the immediate job (the crayon with the greatest value assigned to it). They discover how to organize their collection of crayons in order to achieve the best score in the allotted time.*

I hope you benefitted from these activities!

Conclusion

The various functions our brains carry out that are required for thinking, acting, and problem-solving are collectively referred to by psychologists as executive functioning. Kids' ability to learn new knowledge, retain that information in their thoughts and apply it to solve issues in daily life all fall under the category of executive functioning.

A person can live, work, and study with adequate independence and competence for their age, thanks to their executive functioning skills. People can obtain information, consider options, and implement those solutions.

These abilities do not come pre-developed in children, but they do have the potential to do so. Just like any other abilities, kids can learn executive functioning, some kids can learn them without delays and difficulties, while for others the developmental milestones will be difficult to achieve quickly.

Executive functioning problems vary from kids to kids. Some kids might find it difficult to control their emotions and self-regulate while for some kids the executive functioning problems are related to time management and remembering instructions. Kids with executive function issues frequently find it extremely difficult to become independent and form long-term plans.

Kids executive functioning abilities are affected by various factors including childhood stress and educational odds, but this is a good thing because it implies that executive functioning can be altered and enhanced.

This book is focused on helping parents develop their child's executive functioning skills through practical strategies, activities and worksheets. I hope you have found this book helpful. Children's self-regulation abilities are enhanced by parental and familial support, shared experiences, and quality time spent engaging in commonplace activities like reading, cooking, and dancing. These are unquestionably the most solid and long-lasting executive function pillars.

Strive to thrive with a high level of executive functioning to make the most out of your life!

Made in United States
Troutdale, OR
09/02/2024

22506618R00042